Queen of the Ebony Isles

Wesleyan University Press

Middletown, Connecticut

Queen of the Ebony Isles

Colleen J. McElroy

Other books by Colleen J. McElroy

The Mules Done Long Since Gone

Music from Home: Selected Poems

Winters Without Snow

Lie and Say You Love Me

A Country Under Its Original Name

Some of these poems previously appeared in these magazines or books: *Amazella's Reading List #4* ("The Dragon Lady Considers Dinner," "Alias the Dragon Lady"); *Black Sister: Poems by Black American Women 1746–1980*, Erlene Stetson, ed. ("Ruth"); *Callaloo* ("Runners," "To the Lady Holding the MGM Torch"); *Calyx* ("Monologue for Saint Louis," "Lothar's Wife"); *Cincinnati Review* ("Biography: 1936 to War's End"); *A Country Under Its Original Name*, by Colleen J. McElroy ("A Triangle of Sun Temples and Lost Lakes"); *December* ("Ingredients," "What His Wife Saw," "Pumpkin Eater"); *Greenfield Review* ("Waiting for Answers," "Wake of the Witch Woman"); *Nimrod* ("Why Tu Fu Does Not Speak of the Nubian"); *Ploughshares* ("While Poets Are Watching"); *Poetry Northwest* ("This Is the Poem I Never Meant to Write"); *Rain in the Forest, Light in the Trees: Contemporary Poetry from the Northwest*, Rich Ives, ed. ("A Triangle of Sun Temples and Lost Lakes: After the War of Lost Lakes"); *River Styx* ("Bone Mean"); *Seattle Review* ("Against a Winter of Dreams," "What the Red Flag Means"); *Southern Poetry Review* ("Dreams of Johnson Grass," "From Blue Waters"); *The Third Woman: Minority Women Writers of the United States*, Dexter Fisher, ed. ("Where Iguanas Still Live"); *Willow Springs* ("Queen of the Ebony Isles"); *Woman Poet: The West*, Elaine Dallman, ed. ("Morning in Argentina"). The quotation from Milton Caniff is reprinted by permission of Nostalgia Press.

All inquiries and permissions requests should be addressed to the Publisher, Wesleyan University Press, 110 Mt. Vernon Street, Middletown, Connecticut 06457.

Distributed by Harper & Row Publishers, Keystone Industrial Park, Scranton, Pennsylvania 18512.

LIBRARY OF CONGRESS CATALOGING IN PUBLICATION DATA

McElroy, Colleen J.
  Queen of the Ebony Isles.

  I. Title.
PS3563.A2925Q4 1984 811'.54 84-7494
ISBN 0-8195-5108-2 (alk. paper)
ISBN 0-8195-6101-0 (pbk.: alk. paper)

Manufactured in the United States of America

First Edition

For Makalela Chalk

1927–1979

I would like to thank the National Endowment for the Arts
for a generous grant which made possible the time and travel
needed to write some of these poems.

Contents

III. Queen of the Ebony Isles

I. In My Mother's Room

"Surely I shall keep those who sit on my thighs" but no,
even they, the children of her children were taken from her until it
seemed that she herself was at last to be taken. But no, a change
came over her and she grew younger.

—*The Old Woman Who Tried to Find God*
—South African Folktale

Monologue for Saint Louis

home again and the heart barely there
when choked by clusters of words
thick as the clumps of blue-black
grapes we snitched every summer
from the neighbor's arbor
succulent pockets of flesh laced
with green staining our lips and fingers

it is summer again and I am home
vowing penance for all my disappearances
since that first summer
when the arbor was clotted
with pockets of grapes latticed on each
interlocking vine

now earthworms have trellised the arbor
and that crumbling heap of rotting black
sticks cannot shield us from wind or words
we are the women we whispered about each summer
familiar houses and schoolyards have disappeared
childhood streets are blocked with singular black

one-way signs aligned like a lacework
of warnings or accusing fingers
I am home again
and my cousins sit in their cloaks of black
skin dragging me through twisted vines
of genetic maps thick with childhood vows

they remember each summer
how each year I vowed to return home
forever but I am lost in a riddle of words
home is a vacant lot its back yard clotted
with a stainless-steel arch and clusters
of tiny parks sprouting like trelliswork

enclosing some strange summer
resort my cousins have disappeared
into like the shadows of beasts and bad air
that infect this flat country and I am home
a stranger in love with words
with tart sweet clusters of poems

In My Mother's Room

(for Vanessa)

my mother lies spread-eagle upon the bed
I am in the next room with my daughter
slowly passing away the evening
in a late summer's drone of hours
muffled sounds of children's games
drift through the window
along with the odor of thick honeysuckle
and the flicker of yellow fireflies
the warp and weft of their flight
draws me to the edge of a time when I was
a child, this house my prison
and my mother sprawled naked on the bed
signaled hours to be spent alone
hiding in a book
or in my room under the clapboard eaves
now my father sits by himself in the garden

my mother snores
her mouth open in a sagging *oh*
her flowered bathrobe
slipping from the edge of the bed
in a cascade of roses
I am slumped in the overstuffed chair
watching the TV grind past endless hours
my daughter frowns
but will not look directly at us
fully clothed, I am as vulnerable
as my mother, whose childbearing scars
are slightly visible as she lies under
the humid blanket of another midwestern summer

cankered by antagonisms
we are shadows of black into black
one of the other
I can draw my own body into the damp out-
line she will leave when she awakens
one day, I will walk into this house
lift her flowered robe from my shoulders
then stumble and sink onto that bed
in perfect mimicry
my legs will flow into the age-old patterns
my pubic hairs will curl tightly
into the early evening heat
and I will breathe the labors
of a hundred midwestern summers

but tonight, I am fully clothed
and I smile at my daughter's frowns
she has wrapped herself in innocence
against this scene
I motion her to the door
toward the scent of flowers and children playing
knowing all too soon
she will finally
finger her breasts
and disappear into crowds
of us naked women

Dreams of Johnson Grass

If for a night my tongue would sleep.
—Dara Wier

each night I float into levels of cislunar
space like some weightless astronaut
harvesting dreams that will betray me
if only for a night my mind would sleep
but each night a new world
and landscapes of mysteries
where I orbit inside stories
of family members I've longed to forget

strange shapes blossom and fade
like thickets of brake and nettle
fields of chickweed, stringy mustard
horsetail and crabgrass, once planted
they are fertile but often troublesome
the stingy profiles of next of kin
the generations of distant relatives
creeping home

cousins thrive on the moonscape
of my sleep space
standing in long secular lines
like winter wheat or scrawny maize
their voices raspy as crickets
others are plump as milkweed
and seed my dreams with coarse and pithy
children who call me by my maiden name

Jo-Jo, hey Jo, repeated again and again
in a bed of light, handsome Uncle Phillip
beckons me into his arms
I rush past my mother's clicking tongue
past cross-eyed Cousin Rosa
her frowning face dark as a prune
now my dreamscape is riddled with ghosts
I am Great-aunt Dora jumping trains
outside of Fulton Mo with her bandit lover
or Fanny slumping over the supper table
the shock of poison surprising her heart

I am pulled toward Warren, my eighth-grade love
first cousin removed and no longer
too serious to step across bloodlines
his skin is perfect as obsidian
we finally meet at dawn and I awaken
in the imagined space of his arms
my tongue cannot fill the vacancy with words
they bloom so quickly
these rangy faces from my fragmented past

if only poems could come so easily
so perfectly, like a lock
of white hair above an innocent face
or the meaningless spirals of deep sleep
where I am pure Pulitzer and ride the wind
swirling like pollen
from Solomon's-seal or swaying
above a splendid field of witches'-breath

Ruth

And Ruth said…Intreat me not to leave thee, or to
return from following after thee; for whither thou goest,
I will go….

—Ruth 1:16

it took 27 years to write this poem
27 years mama and still I see you falling
like a lump of coal down a chute
arms hands and feathered thighs churning
inside a tumbling hulk of helpless flesh
falling away from me
your dress flying open
until you were finally free form
and without face

since then I have counted those stairs
I would like to say there were 27
but significance lies not in exactness
but in the panic of not knowing
which step would claim you
I have saved that morning
the blood-sucking thud of body
against wood   the back staircase
of that red brick duplex
where you clawed air

we had fought   I remember that
about what   nothing
grandpa's untimely death
my 16-year-old womanish ways
how someday I too would flail
at my own daughter
so many fights   so many stairs
and you tumbling as my terror
claimed me like Venus
without arms or legs to stop you

one moment you were larger than life
your black arms spread like the wings
of some great vulture   the next a step
missed and you fragile   distorted   plunging
in wingless flight toward some evil nucleus
waiting in the space below the steps
but we cannot go back
I cannot correct that split second
when I failed to lean forward
bodies will not reverse and tumble
upward   unwinding into familiar forms
limbs intact   I have hesitated too long
and the landing is too crowded

what dusty things we would find there now
how you quoted Shakespeare for every event
from slamming doors to Sunday walks and bigotry
a broken lamp   your jealousy and mine
too many unspoken holidays
for your one daughter too many
or too many husbands for one daughter
how your senseless plunge into a void
showed me more than all your ominous warnings
how the cycle of blood and pain
has brought us both to this childless time

I have finally faced myself in you
for years I have written poems nonstop
but yours were always more difficult
I have even tried dream language
but your image slips into some zone
of blackness even deeper in color
than your skin when I angered you

how often has the venom from your blueberry
lips stunted the growth of a poem
how often has your voice been with me
wherever I go   you have gone
and sometimes gladly my need to reach out
has pulled you to me
mama for years I have hidden
hundreds of unfinished verses
in the corners of dark closets

read this
and count them

My Father's Wars

Once he followed simple rules
of casual strength,
summoned violence with the flick
of combat ribbon or hash mark;
now he forces a pulse into treasonous muscles
and commands soap opera villains.
He is camped in a world regimented
by glowing tubes,
his olive-black skin begging for the fire
of unlimited color.
In towns where he can follow
the orders of silence,
gunfights are replayed
in thirty-minute intervals
familiar as his stiff right arm
or the steel brace scaffolding his leg.

By midday the room is filled
with game shows and private eyes hurling
questions against all those who swear
their innocence;
his wife is in full retreat
and jumps when he answers in half-formed words
of single grunts deadly as shrapnel.
He need not remind her
he is always the hero;
the palms of his hands
are muddy with old battle lines.
He has fallen
heir to brutal days where he moves
battalions of enemies;
his mornings are shattered with harsh echoes
of their electronic voices.

Here he is on neutral ground
and need not struggle to capture words
he can no longer force his brain to master;
he plans his roster
and does not attend to his wife's
rapid-fire review of the neighbor's behavior.
He recalls too clearly the demarcation of blacks,
of Buffalo Soldier and 93rd Division.
By late afternoon he is seen rigidly
polishing his car in broad one-arm swipes,
its side windows and bumpers emblazoned
with stickers: US ARMY RETIRED REGULAR

Fishing

and I am standing
          near the water

there's a cold wind
whipping debris across her face
         he waits
           by the tree
               dreaming
         of young warriors
          her lips are set
like bubbles of despair
          her glasses hang
from her neck
         she squints
         into the smoke
         still beautiful
            in the shadows
the cold settles
into a symphony
         of frowns
         she is stirring
            something
into a bent pan
         her black hands
            hiding
         all but the motions
         round and round
         the bitter lines
         circling her pain
          to the quick
he is sitting by the bank
         his gin glass
half full
         half empty
            depending

on his temperament
                he has not caught
                a fish nor looked
                for one since she's
                been his wife
                        yesterday he was Hannibal
or L'Ouverture
                        handsome in his full dress
                                brass, bayonet
and campaign ribbons
                        today he blends
                                into the roots
                        of the old oak
like a black spoor
                he cannot feed
                himself with one
                hand on the line
                the other
                on the glass
so she spoons it in
spilling some
                        the words
                                clanking together
                        like broken marbles
                cat eyes and agates
                so scarred
                they're lackluster
                and no longer
                        sacred
it's a scene in a shoebox
                        played again
and again
                        my mother bending
under the whip
of his words

                    and I
                        in love
                                with my father
    not understanding
                them both

Against a Winter of Dreams

(for Maka)

today it is the hospital again
and all the words that won't matter
I hold your hand and turn my face
toward the window thinking desperately
of stories that will bring you to life
your hand is far too warm
the rain is slick as plastic
and all my stories are full of winter and lead
to children pets and best friends too easily lost

there was that winter I had a fever
my jaw swollen like a rotting gourd
my throat no bigger than a dried tendril of gypsy weed
and the smell of mama's mustard plaster would not diminish
the rain or thoughts of what I imagined
the parade to be despite the starched scout uniforms
hanging green and alone at the far end of the closet
dear sister, how often have we marched since then
our uniforms of skin stretched to cover the years

you told me even bad loves should not die without regret
and now as I watch you easing toward death
I remember how we've sat by so many windows
and like today fought seasons of bitter surprises
while you, dear friend, dance a marathon
of chemicals and cells that multiply too quickly
I have grown to believe all winters
are full of the molting smells of pain
and promises shoved to the far ends of rooms

do you remember the year I gained an orphan
a four-legged wanderer flicked from a moving car
dancer of scarecrow adagios, waddling sideways
into my life like some beige-coated passionate ghost
his eyes filled with posters of starving children
that winter was much like this
and though I fed him, gave him a royal Swahili name
still his thin legs began to twitch with cold grey pain
how quietly now you sleep, slipping into the lull

between the constant retch of constricting muscles
triggered by measured doses of isotopes
did I tell you how as he slept his legs moved
with the old fluid motions of hunter on point
a single gunshot put a stop to that
still at night I think I hear his whimper on the hallway
stairs just as I hear you answer even when you do not speak
inside the slow ticking quiet of this room
sounds have grown into clean acrid smells
now a white uniform tells me this visit is near its end

but we all need to dance when we're awake
to walk beside friends while bands
still play the right anthems
nothing is definite, not you sister
struggling into each breath
not the rib cage pushing against the dacron
thin skin of chest, not my face by the window
round-eyed and alone, remembering all too clearly
too many little things like boxes of trinkets
photos, letters, the way you say my name

While Poets Are Watching

(for Quincy Troupe)

Harlem is on parade
recalling St. Louis
as if like us
the whole scene
has been transplanted here
Stanford White's window offers
remnants of James Van Der Zee's world
it is filled with urgent gospels
infecting us both with memories
of our common birthplace
I see you take notes
always the poet
but in the dry space
where I have stored words
pictures from this Harlem window
kaleidoscope faster
than any pen will move

you have to come back you say
this is rich and heavy
like good food
you say here
are our poems
smiling as your next words
are drowned in tambourines
and harsh songs of salvation
blasting from loudspeakers
lampposted below the window
for a moment the hymns
from the corner tabernacle
outdrum the cadence
of the parade

this is the third Sunday
in August and thirty-second-
degree Masons
strutting like crested pigeons
swell the black heart of this town
we watch from the window
matching faces with memories
the skinny old woman next door
praises the past
like any other church lady
she is powdered like a turn-
of-the-century matron
her sunken black cheeks
dusted with pale blue, ivory or rose
to match pastel dress, stockings, shoes
you take note chanting
come back, come back
this is home and love

we are poets watching
tight-hipped black girls
swing their batons
to the high-step
rhythms of vaseline-smoothed legs
while the oompahs of school bands
count march time for drill teams
we watch until dusk
until the bands
grouped like gaudy flowers
have played their last notes
until the old men have
placed their callused feet
on the nearest footstools
and the girls have gum-chewed
their mothers into silence

20

these faces are familiar
as Van Der Zee's photos
as my mother's snapshots
of cookouts in Uncle Brother's
backyard or your own scrapbook
of our high-school homecoming
it is all predictable
from the street smells
of old whiskey and urine
to the sun fading
against Columbia's canker-
green roof
we are home, coming back
always coming back

Runners

we called it scrammin'
and all niggers were targets
Franklin Newport Washington, Jr.
could outrun a cop
on a 2.4-mile stretch
could get hat and scab too

now the joggers
lope past my window
like wild deer in season
leisurely heading for some salt lick
on a nearby wilderness trail

they bug me
running without purpose or fear
running until their hearts burst
and their sweat turns sweet

when old Franklin whipped by
slick as soaped skin
we always knew his pounding heart
and bulging eyes signaled a flash
of blue less than half a block away

if it wasn't Franklin
it was Ernestine Dupont
caught in a hustle
her slit skirt hiked up over her knees
and panic pulled tight across her face

and them old church ladies
sitting behind the safe corners
of their hand-crocheted curtains
would talk about wild kids
sin and hell
never saying a damn thing
about body conditions

Bone Mean

it is easy to believe she's primordial
and will last forever
I have seen her stalk a single cockroach
ferreting on point until the crusty brown
body lies belly up
she says by instinct they're too bold
but this is her way with all things
when I was eight I loudly proclaimed
a great distaste for green mints
the next year she stacked my birthday
in verdant layers
cake cookies napkins ice cream
in shades of green from moss to myrtle
mint to emerald beryl to apple
bottle and fir
all reflected in sickly tints
against my black cheeks
in church she sings gospels with a vengeance
amening the preacher whose small black face
too often reminds her of the husband
she's tried to bury beyond memory
every family has one
an old woman whose bile grows more bitter

who raises strong spinsters
shuffling their days like Tarot cards
full of evil signs
she has stacked the world
against her daughters
now those girls ring her house like trees
fat stumps of hardwoods evergreens deciduous
their voices spiderwebbing their mother's
words into exacting patterns
their own words buried years ago
now petrified and turned into stone
six layers of lipstick and strong perfume
keep them ageless
but she wants them hard and mean
as Triassic fossils
she is relentless and will not rest
until she has pruned and pinched
them into bonsai symmetry
until they believe without any doubt
that she brings all life to earth

Where Iguanas Still Live

(for Kevin)

This is what is important
A first birthday picture
The rubber bathtub toy
Clutched in your fat fingers
You giggly and myopic
How important it was
When you locked all the doors
Three years old
And instant master of the house
Outside I danced to your amusement
A black Natasha snowbound
And twirling in a web
Of my own desperation
How fragile it seems when years
Cannot release us
The mystery of time
Is not important
One night you said Mama
I can hear the whistles blowing
Then still asleep
You walked away from me

You are out there now
A man walking quickly
To another shore
I am here where
Knights and their ladies still romp
Through your storybooks
You helped your sister
Learn the alphabet
Tracing the mystery of each letter
Now your posters of African kings
Curl like delicate petals
In the corner of the closet
They are still strong and willing
To hunt lions in the tall grass
It is here we keep time
The carefully measured ticking
Like watching buds grow

We planted corn seeds
Inside freezer bags
Experiments in temperature you said
Quietly proud and so serious
I enrolled you in a club
An animal a month delivered by mail
Fish lizards mice
Jelled dehydrated beheaded
Laced with ink from overdue bills
And letters from your grandmother
Later you stood on the abyss of my anger
While baby snakes nested warm
Inside half-filled cosmetic jars

It is important that even now
Though you are not here
I remember how we groped
Hand in hand in the dark
Softly calling the iguana
Lost forever
Inside the pattern of the Persian rug.

From *Homegrown*
An Asian-American Anthology of Writers

I have seen this picture before
usually after a war
it is always faded brown-grey
and slightly burned around the edges
the composition is much the same
eyes full of innocence trying
vainly to guard young bodies
the boy in front is the leader
and the couple there
deliberately not holding hands
are lovers
they are all poets

they are always standing on the stairs
of some building where accordingly
they learn by generation
what lines have brought them there
the sun always washes
their various sizes with a hopeful blur
they are always the ones who want
to knit the old country to its children
and they are the ones who steal for a free
breakfast bags of oranges and cookies
for preschoolers and old ladies
who smile their appreciation

this picture holds names that are Asian
but it is much like those I've seen
on reservations or one my mother has
of me near Selma with friends
from my all-black high school
or maybe my younger brother
before his uniform was official
in this picture and the others
it is the last recognizable day

before the hills take what we know
to be our childhood
and that girl on the right will
no doubt walk a barefoot snow trail
to death and the intellect will
gain hostility with each
point of lost logic
and the writer will find
no metaphors in bullets
and their own people will
finally understand them even less
than the rest of the world

A Sight for Sore Eyes

Under a sky speckled with gulls
keening for saltier air,
drunks here acknowledge splendid light
draping the pergola and carry their lives
around like plots from movies that could only
be filmed in the city that coined *Skid Road*.
Each one has a story or two
borrowed for a moment of wine and if luck
holds something stronger to run in the fog
where all dreams become lies in the telling.

Out here tourists beckon without looking,
braving the underground tour
so they can boast to folks back in Duluth,
Delaware or Dexter just what's to be had
in the damp pits of lower Seattle.
Aboveground derelicts stumble and smile
straight on for the cameras —
after five seconds of eye contact,
they will drape you in fumes
of ambitious secrets or fake childhoods.

One carries a mottled copy of *Catcher
in the Rye* in his back pocket
and will recite passages for quarters;
another sporting a scar that pulls
his mouth into a pucker of raw flesh
claims he flew bees in his youth,
tied the big fuzzy ones to string
and gave them their lead
like dive bombers on secret missions,
and the one who too quickly poses
for instant snapshots
grins only from the right and yells
have a nice day, fucker,
then thumb-picks his nose.

I have watched scenes like these unfold
through the whole of postcard afternoons—
tourists circling Pioneer Square like relatives
holding deathwatch over some codger's sickbed.
They wait for something to happen
and normal as rain it does.
An Indian ten years into his decay
has fallen for a lady too old for luck;
he drops to one knee in a Romeo's plea,
the movement so honest we all turn away,
but love, drunk or sober, fits hand
in glove and never wonders what fool
first invented kissing.

I remember how folks in my neighborhood
said a man could lie down in the gutter
one day and rise up sweet the next
but still I have been trained
to hold fast to distance among beggars,
to never look at shadows in doorways or alleys
and so, like the others, I turn or stare
at nothing no matter what the cause.
I shuck off easy recognition
of stomach-wrenching bums who wink and tell
me black girls have cinnamon centers, and me
grinning smugly at the colors of those words.

But this rings too close to home, familiar
as Saturday nights and families held together
by stories they'd soon as not hear—like the old
hands who line park benches and smile like uncles
during their tourist versions of whiskey-soaked tales.
Little of any day captures their full attention—
the bronze of Seattle sunsets or sleek ferries
docking in unison at the foot of old logging trails;
the sightseers who believe decency is above
all this, and like me, blinded for a moment by the sun
laughing against plate-glass windows,
watching as all of our reflections fail us.

II. In Any Language

A wolf, peeping through a window, saw a company of shepherds eating a joint of lamb. "Lord," he exclaimed, "what a fuss they would have raised had they caught me doing that."

—*Aesop's Fables*

A Triangle of Sun Temples and Lost Lakes

1. Among the Sun Temples

These mountains are like women.
From a distance they are soft, graceful and willing,
Their skirts neatly arranged
As if they are following some pattern.
These stately ladies
Attended the River of the Sun
Even before it gained its name.
From Pachácamac to Sacsahuamán
They have embraced Quechua and Inca,
They are willing to embrace you.
Like mothers they will harbor you,
Bring you fruit, bread, the juice of rare leaves.
They will shelter virgins
And shove strong boys into manhood.
At night you can sleep
In the crevice of their bosoms.
They will whisper strange stories
Of the moon and stars
But do not trust them,
They will pinch your ears
With the pain of thin air
Or drown you in crystal-clear waters.
They have conquered gods
And men who would treat them like midwives.
Yet they always beckon,
Sucking the wind into their cleavage
In a lonesome harlot's song,
Their tawdry green dresses
Full of sensuous mystery.
They have been kissed by centuries of history,
By Inti, Sinchi and jewel of Quechua.
They are called all mountain—all peak,
Navel of sun god, flesh of inner earth.
And while they hold the surprise

Of innocent young daughters,
They have grown hard as adulterous wives.

2. After the War of Lost Lakes

Under a soft celestial quilt
The beggars outside Lima
Curl up in the warm dust of yesterday.
Though it smells of lost lakes and llamas,
Strong warriors and the bowels of ancient gods,
It does not close out the cold mountain air
Or memories of the great halls of Machu Picchu,
So they buzz like ragged hummingbirds
Against the pale rims of small bonfires.
On the Urubamba they were keepers
Of lovely women and sun-blessed kings.
Now a ten-gauge railroad
Zigzags through their dreams
While church bells peal in chorus.
They sleep in layers,
The old ones nearest the cobblestones
Their eyes falcon sharp
And bloated with hunger,
Their bones brittle as Pizarro's
Whose parchment-colored corpse
Is preserved at even temperature
Inside the cathedral behind them.
These are the true relics of saints,
These gaunt creatures who beg
In the shadows of trees,
Whose ancestors carved their names
On the bloodstained walls of catacombs.
Here in the square where geography is locked
In pottery, bones, and snakes,
Their tortured past has been made
Part of the national monument.

This is the legend.
It is in their eyes
And each morning when they arrange
Tattered pieces of their history
Into gaudy tourist patterns,
Then welcome the sun
Back to the town
They still call Pisac,
You can see them jangle
Their conquerors awake
With a vengeance.

3. Mirrors in Ecuador

Today we leave for Otavalo—
We will shop for emeralds, ruanas,
And bread-dough figures of Christ.
The weather here is home—
A macramé of lakes knots valleys to mountains.
In the crevices towns spread like plankton.
This is a northwest scene painted Spanish.
We will consume its treasures.
On each corner we will capture street vendors.
Every morning they blossom like bright flowers,
Their birdlike chatter
Filling the spicy air.
Behind their shields of humility
They sing out to us—
For you, madame, this is special.
This is the offer for which you will pay.
You will smile when clever natives
Swallow your money like aspirin.
I season my peppered nerves with poetry
While the others shield themselves
Behind cameras and zippered bags.
My skin offers no shield.

Here among Pasalaquas, Mestizos, and Creoles
I am too much at home.
Here where the rain blows
Into the hollows of sun-ruffled valleys,
Where hillsides dip and swirl like green velvet
Or wrinkle like the fleshy thighs
Of huge dark women,
I watch my twin barter for gold.
In the liquid shadows her blackness is familiar—
But I am called madame
And for her I am special.
When she praises my one-line Spanish
Her eyes are hungry for dollars.
She is Esmeralda selling tribal dreams
Of green fire—
She has been here before
And knows the power of bargaining,
But all I see in the space between words,
Between drops of rain
Is how we are both sad
In any language.

Morning in Argentina

(for Helen Shapiro)

poems in hand, I follow
Helen's camera
from the carbon-soaked hillsides
of Zipaquirá
to the Plaza San Martín
where cobblestones are ancient
as death

we no longer trust what we see
tourist hotels
are legal as government houses
their palisades so full
of civilized glory
we almost fail to see
the famous poet tracing hedgerows
of trailing vines with his white cane

the camera records the scene
and for one second
Borges is frozen in a cloak of bright
Sunday colors
while pigeons walk with a child's innocence
their up-and-tuck steps
reflected in murky ripples of shallow puddles
their chalky eyes blindly tilted
toward the West

only the poor
choke in this land of good air
picture postcards are filled
with boleros and tanned leathers
while the stark white domes of cathedrals
bleed into shadows
of battle-ready guns

Borges, what do you see with your inner eye
a personal anthology of Indian names
in a town where all the Indians have vanished
a riot of imaginary beings romping
in the lush green of Amazon fables
anything but the actual scene
the prophesy of lands where fallen leaves
stare at us with dead eyes
where birds will not weave
our memories into morning

What the Red Flag Means

This is no Spanish dream
In this town, they glean rough wool into rugs
Madonnas are carved from sandalwood
Their smiles eternally fragrant
The red flag signals fresh meat
And the thick sweet smell of blood

Peasants and gentry surge
Toward the town's center
Their smiles glazed by the odor
Of entrails and sinewy muscles streaming
In the sunlight of the butcher's doorway
I am trapped in the marketplace

Caught in a funeral procession
For some third grader
Who stood too close to the blade
The bull's head lies on the cobblestones
The child's face still trapped in its eyes

This is how they do it
One smooth cut
And the crowd licks at Spanish words
For life and death
While mourners weave past
Like cherubs in school clothing

The wood-carver works faster
Chips falling to the dirge
Of a dozen tiny feet as he whittles
Precise contours of the casket
Miniature faces, the bull's head
The cup and curve of Peruvian mountains

The red flag wavers, is still
And behind the cracked shutters
Of the last house on the square
A black face stares at me
Under this dull Peruvian sun
Our eyes will not hold

The soft curl of the carver's blade
We still remember diaspora
Conquistadors and human heads rolling
And how we've both arrived here
All at once and at the same time

This is what the red flag means
My black face even darker
In the shadows of this town
That other face caught in a window
While on the end of the blood-raw neck
The bull's head swells inside
The green mold of death

This Is the Poem I Never Meant to Write

my grandmother
raised me Georgia style
a broken mirror
spilled salt
a tattered hemline
all add up to bad spirits
when she died, I learned to worship
stranger things
a faded textbook full of bad theories
has no spirit at all
now I've gone full circle
in a town some still call Bahía
the drumbeat of the alabés
echoes my grandmother's warnings
I watch the daughters of the candomblé
dance to the rhythms of ancient spirits
as the ceremony begins
my lungs expand
like gas-filled dirigibles
stretched latex-thin

my grandmother spoke
the language of this scene
the mystery and magic
of rich colors in a tapestry
of brown and black skin
white candles
a small reed boat
six bloody gamecocks
all bind this church to its African source
I follow my people past spirit houses
past tight Spanish streets
where houses are painted blue and white
like any Moorish town
when we reach the sea
water seems to flow uphill
tropical landscapes turn mustard yellow
and above us the moon swallows the night

this is the poem
I never meant to write
I am learning to worship
my grandmother's spirits
an old woman
splinters of wood embedded
in her black leathery cheeks
three crosses tattooed
on the fleshy black skin
of her upper arms
draws my picture upon her palm
in blue ink
then tells me we are all strangers
bound by the same spirit
I have gone home
in the dim light
my grandmother smiles

Cutting a Road from Manaus to Belém

the Amazon peeled back to gold and rubber
the clink of coins more definite than the purulent
yellow of common colds and aboriginal hunger

Xingu bankers thumbing gilded bills
mouthing numbers like thick throat
mints peppering mud-fevered palates

the green everybody wants, eyeball
blade-edged, cucumber-new green

land robbers shimmering cobalt on camera
faces bloating like seafoam backwash
of graph-green images

movietone civilizados wallowing
in wealth, their wives long in the tooth
and up to the neck in emeralds and bad luck

potent jealousy of have and have-not, of defoliating
for the sake of money in air too thick to breathe
voice-overs spitting Mato Grosso credit card power

the earth's heart-belt of mold, madness and business
names of lost tribes full of x's, j's, and double l's
surrounding a one-lane road named progress

the bait of big bucks, the white man's duty, the one good
turn of being in the *Black*—yeah

the challenge, my little chickadee,
the go-for-it of greenhorns, of slick
palms and mossy dollar bills

From Blue Waters

it is summer and windsocks are poppies
fluttering in the warm breezes
off the Gulf Stream
we throw nets
dyed green to match the sea
gulls float on stagnant air
and the oil slick has drifted
beyond the twenty-mile limit

each year the whales swim past
like time travelers
in cuneiform precision
this year man-made parasites
hold fast to humpbacks and greys
until they lose their bearings
and mouths as wide as canyons
dive for land

like fast-forward flashes of evolution
they are out of control
finally falling victims
to rhapsody of the deep
their cracked sonars of sound
no longer locate objects by echo
but they need no microscope
to confirm the details
like Icarus they are in trouble
and they know it

on the beach their bodies pock the sand
like grey metal hulks of rusting ships
caramel glazed eyes shed grease
but the air is free of brine
I'd like to say I'm concerned
only with corporate matters
or that I've married a Jesus freak
and live in South Dakota raising
a passel of kids and six nanny goats
or that my fourth cousin is no longer bound
by the blackness of St. Louis ghettos

but filigrees of light dance
against the whales' bodies
and barnacles calcify in the dry air
like a lady's jewels
we have all been lost
my cousin who moved to South Dakota
only to find that families of goats
graze on chemically parched grass
in all midwestern states
these whales who wait

for the sea to roil with their blood
their cries squeaking across the sand
like door hinges or blind kittens
they stop and it is real as stone
and it is earth and it is flat
and it goes on for miles

The Point of No Return

In the Azores the wind screams like a child
who's been cheated out of his turn at bat;
Portuguese dream of land
and Army transports carry blacks to two continents.
This picture has been trapped in my mind for years;
it has always been this way.
When Equiano's black face turned west
his shackles clanged like bells
and the sea was cradled in the same white froth.
Now on that small spit of land at the point
of no return Torre de Belém tall as a demon
still glares at the emerald waters
and tides still ring a death toll
against its castle-grey walls.

Blacks line the shores facing the cold
of northern countries and dreaming of the tropics.
I dream of home where my father's weapons
mark him a strong warrior;
his Eighth Army ribbons plastered against his chest
flat and shiny as algae.
My passport stamps me free of slavers
but I still smell fear in the air.
Here there is no turning back.
Portuguese traders still strip the flesh
from large fish and gather citrus
but we have outlived the days of long voyages;
now jets slide away from the ragged cliffs
like evil drones awash in deadly noise.

Twice each day they swoop once over the rotting
moorings below the castle's mouth
then scream toward the west;
Europe lies to the east.
Soldiers, blacks, and tourists are balanced
for weight while fish and fruit add ballast.
Strapped in my seat I see the islands below me
grow smaller as the sea licks shadows
from the edges of porthole windows;
morning is a thin silver light.
The new world awaits
and I am bound to its life.

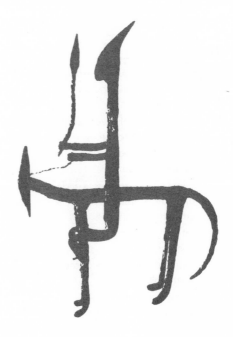

The Last Outpost Before Point Roberts

Back home my father has hung
his rifle over the bedroom door,
my mother's chair is flanked
by two artillery shells—
silent sentries filled with sand
and aimed for invisible targets.
Out here gun emplacements
are gaping holes
pointing toward the sea.
I stare through their open mouths,
imagine awesome targets
barely visible on the horizon—
when I pull back, the wind
sucks through mourning countless deaths.
My Piscean friend says
forget the past
but this place conjures up
my father's boots,
spit-shined and standing ready
in the hallway—
his black face lost in a troopload
of starched khaki soldiers
while I wander
into new schools every season,
facing the awesome task
of a new language.
My friend says
collect sea air and sand dollars
but anchors and cannons
clutter my vision.
Out here even the graffiti
fall victim—
on the concrete walls of the bunker,
two rhinos copulate
leering like enemy tanks.
This place could be Fort Hood,

Dawson or Riley—
exchange the gulls
for cactus and crab grass.
Housing is standard U.S. Army,
soaking in civilians
like litmus paper.
Always the parade grounds are dead
center so no one can lose sight
of the target—
and always the cemeteries
mark the final boundaries.

Waiting for Answers

you need your ears to find your way in the dark
a ringing phone startles you quickly as any predator
coming alive only at night and seldom at close range
at night you are cautious and full of warnings
your eyes open red and wary of snares in the walls

the voices inside your head fail to fill the room
your bones hold the scan of small animals in negative print
the only true sounds are digital clocks or wailing firetrucks
you cannot find the phone and even your heart and breath
will not proclaim this home as their own

your arms waver toward any sound
fluttering in the cavern of a reverse dawn
like the wings of the fruit bat
in the first moments of awakening

like the bat all voices you hear are on radar
so your skin stretched like silk over the long bones of forearms
gives rise to what most people dread
does it matter that you feel safer inside the sweet moss
of your sheets while other creatures hum toward bright light?

does it matter that the operator's accent is spanish
that she proclaims this an emergency?
does it matter that the call is long distance and will not
translate into numbers you wish to forget?

you are imperfectly warmblooded and in the smooth flat
    blackness
your squeaking lungs widen, begging for conversation
you assure her the line is clear, you will accept the charges
and when the slippery soft silence once again covers the walls
you lie there, repeating the names, all the nouns and verbs
the echoes that signal the limits of your world

Wake of the Witch Woman

I meet the sun's grains eye
to eye, and they fail at my closet of glass.
Dead, I am most surely living....
    —James Dickey, "The Sheep Child"

I briefly read the first news item
thinking it of little human interest
bodies disappear from mortuaries
so infrequently and are forgotten
the intervening days gathered
like gravel in the corners of my eyes
one week later a second item
a second disappearance
the persistence of this dead thing
the grains of dust
linking mortuary to mortuary
across town   across freeway by-passes
parks and indoor tennis courts
built on civic improvement loans
the sun groveling for a space
between menacing grey clouds
the body fully clothed
appearing and disappearing
from embalming rooms and licensed
homes for the dead
the hair now filled with grit
too unkempt and unruly for a wake
until the story slips from page one
to ten to thirty and the personals
and the grandchildren
keening on street corners
like news vendors
    where is the corpse
    where is the corpse

has she found that space in the clouds
that direct route where she flies
like a witch screaming
        I have taken matters into my own
        hands   my veins stiff and filled
        with your chemicals   I travel
        the west wind   for years
        I have yearned for this bloodless
        time   thirty-five years
        punctuated by angry clots
        every twenty-eight days
        each month I gave
        seldom whining
        but always I served
        am I not like the barmaid in Munich
        who at fifteen donated
        sandy yellow urine to a gnarled
        scientist so that the world
        could have barbiturates
        or the slave girl who gave
        without lifting her black head
        from the shingled wood of a dusty
        cabin floor   am I not the whore
        smirking in the sad corner
        of some shady hotel's lobby

or the fat red-faced farm woman
pinned against the mattress of hay
deep in a drought-stricken county
was I not at my best then
or later when men took from me
more than I cared to offer
even married I was
perfectly packaged
when he came from behind
and above in movements
like love   I was confined
producing   always producing
and now finally dead
the cramped space of a coffin
offers no freedom
so I must rise from this dark house
and meet the sun's grains
eye to eye

An Altered State of Awareness

> *They offer me their stories*
> *And I drink an architecture of myth.*
> —Margaret Shafer, "Waiting"

Three photographs on the wall
Signed to you—love as always
I have lived in infinitives
To see to touch to kiss
In the first photo I own time
I am eighteen and womb fresh
Daddy's girl dreaming of fires exploding
The flames are bouquets
Poppies and roses gathered just for me
Close up my face bends in rounded angles
It is flesh and earth—the poet's poem
And glimmers on the flat surface of the film
My blackness is honed like a fine jewel
My teeth as perfect as sunlight
In the next frame
My eyes hold dreams of endless space
I am thirty and all there is
Is love

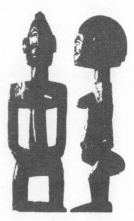

I am lost inside myself
Each tightly curled hair
Vibrates to a sensuous tune
I am a black snake veiled and perfumed
Undulating on the tip of a sweet man's horn
Its songs whisper commands
Lovely lady trapped in the blues
You will learn to dance
Climb inside the deep song of my jazz trumpet
It is behind your eyes
The softer I play it
The stronger it gets—I drink every note
And wondering who's woman I am
Believe it is the only sound
I have come to know
Until the last photo where I am older
Embrace bright silence
And do not answer to age

I stare at these pictures for hours
I cannot bury their ghosts
Three images offer fragments of my life
Close up they are haunted by love
And gaze upon each other
Decades apart and full of myth
I have seen reasonable monsters
The rhythms of their bodies
Are gathered in lines around my mouth
Infinities have eclipsed time
And all melodies now call me to the sea
To live to know to love
Now nested in the dark part of the universe
I am one with myself—content to be
Neither happy nor unhappy
Smiling and dreaming of pictures
That no longer seem to resemble anything

III. Queen of the Ebony Isles

We sailed many days and nights, and we passed from isle
to isle and sea to sea and in due course, came upon an
island as it were a garth of the gardens of Paradise.
—*Selections from the Arabian Nights,* "Tales of Scheherazade"

Why Tu Fu Does Not Speak of the Nubian

she draws fat birds
in strokes tight as geography
their plump bodies
arch above bent twigs and flowers
in a splash of boneless color
remember the leaves and veins she says
Chinese painting captures the spirit
the character of space
the observer looks down
stresses only foreground
the use of line gives substance
to the motion
these contours fall into simple patterns
like Tu Fu's poems
easy she says watching my brush
tremble toward the paper
but it is difficult
these fat birds and simple bamboo stalks

they have no urban counterparts
I want to fill the space
with fat black babies
with the veined hands of wretched old men
and big mamas in flowered dresses
shying away from welfare lines
the slender fingers of these thin twigs
should bend to the sweet pain
of old love songs played on
clear water and clean rocks
should ease the sullen jokes
of schools gone bad
while colors blend like Ashanti rhythms
played on Osebo's drum
draw them many many times she says
they grow from the mind without roots
so I bend over porcelain-white paper
remember to pull all lines toward the center
and always the dark into light

To the Lady Holding the MGM Torch

Before I met poets
who spoke jealously
of each other's lovers
I watched my loves unwind
from the tight cold black reels
of a hundred Saturday matinees
in the darkness
I was without color
while ribbons of flesh
so wonderously woven
into quick blonde kisses
and hermetic sunsets
became larger than life

I fashioned a costume
from vivacious eyelashes caught
in the suspense of a single moment
gained membership to planets
where I lived
on the strength of a single letter
I still remember those halting
lines so full of secret formulas
and sex fading into the chromacolor
of harpsichord and violin

now in dark rooms
they rest at celibate temperatures
the canned laughter
the Dead End kids
my old loves and I
I see obituary notices
of cancerous growths and failing
hearts but I wait
for their revival
and on the late night movies
I am Lena Horne diaphanously floating
in the fast frame of a stormy sky

I pull their words
into gramophonic moans
and fight the dawn with heavy eyelids
just to see that last scene
that last sigh and firm chin
the hero's callused hand
raised to caress the perfect face
of some hard-edged lady
brassy with youth
once again I am eighteen
and anxious
who is to know we have all grown
soft and dimpled with patience

Queen of the Ebony Isles

this old woman follows me from room to room
screams like my mother   angers like my child
teases me   rolling her tattooed hips forward
and out   steals my food   my name   my smile
when you call her I come running

when we were young and perfect
we danced together and oh we loved well
all the husbands and lovers   children and books
the sunshine and long walks on lonely nights
now she sucks me thin with her affairs

weaves romantic shadows over the windows
and curses my sober moods   kisses everyone
and insists on wearing red shoes
she hums the same songs over and over
something about love and centuries turning upon us

each time she changes the verse
shifting the words like cards in a game
of solitaire   the hot patent-leather colors
her mercurial moods as she flies about
her red heels glittering and clicking out of tune

she has seen too many comic strips
believes she's as deadly lovely
as Dragon Lady and Leopard Girl   I resist
but her limbs are daring   oiled for movement

without me who are you she asks   I am heavy
with silence   my hands are maps of broken lines
without her all sounds are hollow   I am numbed
cold and cannot read the cycles of the moon
even the sun   the sun cannot warm me

aloneness is a bad fiddle I play against my own
burning   bet your kinky muff she cackles knowing
the symptoms   then draped in feather boas
she drags me toward yet another lover   beckoning
with her brash reds pulsing like haunting violins

on midnight-blue nights she screams
into the eyes of the moon   twirling her war machine
like some Kamikaze pilot   her heat bakes my skin
even blacker   she's never happy unless we're falling
in love or hate   she grows younger while I

age and age   bandage wounds and tire too easily
she says   play the game   play the game she says
when I complain she says I'm hearing voices
she's hacked my rocking chair into firewood
I am the clown in all her dreams

when she looks into the mirror from my eyes
I want to float away unscathed
drift like patches of early morning fog
she thinks I stay because I love her
one day soon I'll move while she's sleeping

The Ghost-Who-Walks

none of this makes any sense
not if you consider
what you really remember
not the name of the high yella
snooty kid third row front seat
who sat like an eraser
September to June for three
grades with her clean name
long hair and starched shirts
and your mama called her uppity
and all you can remember
is how often the teacher called
her and how you hated
the way she made your sad
face seem dirty

so why should you remember
some cheap comic hero
who never looked like any man
you knew then or since
or could talk to or sing to
those silly songs
about freckle-faced
sweethearts who never lived
on your block or wars
you never fought
or black folks full of voodoo
that made your gramma laugh
and throw salt over her shoulder
or women who pined and waited
for men like you
never have or will

none of this has anything really
to do with the way bright-
eyed children gather shadows
of words and make pictures
and run with them
the way the Phantom ran from Sala
to Diana and back again
and how he always said
darkness was good and goodness
was light and the pygmies
howled and cringed and he
marked his victims with a skull
which we all have

Ingredients

remember you need a hero
preferably orphaned or somehow lost
and a symbol, some cross
to bear on cross-country treks
there will be lots of traveling
and talk of love
but the woman must be weak, frail
and prone to trouble
or else how will the hero
make use of his calling
and how else will he properly flex
the cunning muscles of his brain
and what else could draw him back
to his mythical kingdom?

take for instance the Phantom
skull ring and grey tights
mark his presence
full grown he lopes through forest
and city alike exposing himself
to sordid characters
without regard for the love
of one Diana Palmer
but only to make our lives safer
meanwhile back in Bandar
his faithful blackamoors wait
for their master
get the picture?

not quite because as usual
something is missing
in this case the hero dies
his grey dog howls, the moon grows
dull, the blue parrot's voice is still
and you are ready for the last frame
the final episode
but wait old Diana is giving birth
colors bleed from her profile
in one final gasp
the other women, dark Liana
and deviously shaded Sala
shed one single tear
then add more years to their lives
while good, pale fair-haired Diana expires
now what does that tell you?

Lothar's Wife

he's only a smart-ass when he's home
with Mandrake
he's silent and obedient as a snail
his bald pate bowing into the cape's
trail and dreaming
of tales he'll bore me with
his one night home

once a month
that's what I get like clockwork
and always on the full moon
half my allowance he reserves
for sheets, tearing them with his teeth
to vent the forced silence
of those other twenty-odd days

did I say odd
it's that one day that's odd
his coming home full of half-tricks
he's picked up from the master
the hypnotic hunger
he so willingly tries on me
he claims he stole me, bought me

claims he's Zulu, Bantu, Beja
depending on the hour, day, or year
says I was the black spot
in the white of his eye
the speck he turned into leopard
that unwittingly turned into woman
neither of us no longer knows what's real

and my mother beats her fat tongue
against her gums
as each month I try to reveal the puzzle
stroking the lines from his hairless
obsidian crown
I hear her rumbling around in the next room
I soothe his sweet head and she moans
heaven protect us from all the things
to which we can become accustomed

Letters from Distant Kingdoms

dear mother, I have not written
for a year and the winds have blown
me far from home
Lothar stays on the run
a child or two tucked under each arm
while I am gathered in the wake
of stories about his Herculean strength
what else can I report

because Narda admired his thin cheeks
and the way water beads on the long muscles
of his back like bright pebbles lining
the west shore of the Zambezi River
he suddenly became Yoruba
refused to eat my corncakes
and told me his kingdom was east
of the Volta

when I mumbled by way of Harlem no doubt
and mentioned how Narda
was once a traitor
he threatened to paint a spit curl
on his forehead and move to the mountains

because Mandrake saw him standing tall
as a Fulani between fake walls of fire
and beasts turning into men
he has now moved his kingdom due west
wears a fez and refuses
to speak of leopard skins

like any good wife
I have turned my own hypnotic gestures
into fine recipes for sweet
cakes and mornings without prayer

one night in Harlem with Mandrake's
illusions still dancing in his eyes
he shifted his roots south of the Sudan
muttered whole sentences
doodled Tibetan chants on my shoulders
and imagined himself with hair

three toes on his left foot
have been broken and reset
at least eight times
now he can't count past seventeen
yet each year he plays with images of shoes
weaving their shadows like old silk scarves
or tired rabbits pulled from his birthday hat

I am his trusty assistant nodding
suggestively at double-laced boots
nail-studded heels or cordovans
pulling boxes from shelves as if trapped
in a vanishing act gone berserk
I am wife-mistress, bitch-magician, woman-
sawed-in-half and the trick is to be lovingly
accusing as I feed my own whining

mother, each year it is the same
he is still silent and bald
and I have learned to eat all sins
until he himself is without guilt
home becomes more distant
I add more palm kernels
to the sweet cakes
our laughter attracts
the jackals

What His Wife Saw

he practices with an old cape
hides furtively behind its folds
like a ghetto criminal on the dodge
his eyes take that mean and slanty look
but it's all out of synch
even his name does not fit
I would have like Eddie or Clifford
but Mandrake insisted on Lothar
now we're stuck

he says he is a desert warrior
a leopard in manskin
a nomad freed from jungle trails
he says he will pull the master's
magic back into the blackness
of rain-forest shadows where it belongs
but his thick fingers cannot paint
symbols of earth
and his shoulders refuse to hold
the folds of a cape

because he believes magic precedes
the tilling of soil
he rinses himself in vapors
from smoking leaves
and waits to hear me whisper tales
lifted from the craters of the moon
or weave soft songs like ribbons
but even for a world of illusions
he is asking too much
it has all been too much

one hypnotic gesture too many
one magician too many
too much of his bald head bobbing
his arms waving like branches
of the sparrow tree
no matter how long he stares
at the red-brown clay of ostrich cups
no matter how much he mutters
he loves me I will not ask the keeper
of dreams to render his ancestors real

I know he believes I hold all of Nubia's
soapstone secrets but he is tied
to the wrong master
silently watching swirls of single patterns
and tracing incisions feathered
along the rim of the amphora in a slicing
glissando even Mandrake has come to envy
if for once he would listen before leaping
in to rescue the same tired act
I would tell him how finally
all stories fall like stones
how sometimes all we need is visibly held
in the cusp of an oval bowl

Pumpkin Eater

sixteen years I've listened
to his awful dialect
a gumbo mixture of central-
casting nightmares
it resembles no region
on earth
you do work he says
then brings me animals
trapped in nameless cages
their stomach-wrenching smells
flood the house
and my garden is filled
with special foods
none of us will eat

you make day move he says
his limpid black eyes
like two dots magically
transferred from his loincloth
but I need more than leopard skin musk
his quick embrace and those eternal
cups of thick coffee he leaves
like old cowrie shells
in these hollow rooms
always Mandrake's visit highpoints
the week and I'm expected
to sit in the corner nodding
while they play with illusions
like guitarists on center stage

he says make babies don't grow fat
me peaceful fella me go now Bandar
I wave goodby to puffs of dust
left by his bare feet
the sun is streaked with shadows
trailing Mandrake's cape
the children are camped on beaches
the animals squeal as I close
the cage doors
these are the days I try
writing poems
but there are no words that rhyme
with Lothar damn you Lothar

Alias the Dragon Lady

(for Peter)

actually Dragon Lady
is just a name
any face will do
I've stolen pieces of this one
from washerwomen full of primordial defiance
like the rough side of mountains
facing the open sea
years later even ragged lines are velvet
once a poet with a camera
stalked me through a hotel lobby
I showed him no face you could recognize
told him pay attention to details
and never mind the color
whatever you think I might be
is better than any explanation I can offer
I've sold these plans to countries
full of heroes
never showing my morning face
all innocence and open as a lover's palm

by evening my mirror reflects
a wide blank space where I fill in names
and places as exotic as you wish
caped in mystery and always devious
I become the painter so involved in art
I begin to understand myself
I am the hustler pulling the greatest trick
of the century on the late night movie
the hooker caught in a trick on the corner
in New York Hong Kong Chicago rain
I have costumes for each one
I am the young girl waiting for first love
balancing loneliness against her English theme
I will do accurate imitations of my mother
so eerie she becomes my daughter
I become in turn my banker my doctor
my telephone and house full of rituals
my thousands of look-alike sisters
I am only the other side of the coin
a voice buzzing inside your head all day long

How She Remembers the Beginning

I woke up just in time to clear my throat
it was like the ending to an old rerun movie
the hero had been buried
one engine conked out over the Aleutians
shrimp had stopped feeding on the west shore
and some fool was trying single-handedly
to clean up Harlem
I materialized in one complete stanza
a distortion of memory like a seance
of poetry or a broken record playing
Angel Baby again and again
an inscrutably haunting tune
warbling against a cracked needle
I became a hustler a thief
stole these lines from old dusty comics
I found in an abandoned barn
stole them all from a time when dreams
were medicinal and the world was full
of mystery and love

but this is only a fragment of my story
originally my plan included saving the world
now I must save only myself
empires have risen because of a woman
and fallen for the same reason
a Dragon Lady recognizes her weaknesses
only sentiment can lower the iron mask
of my reserve
there is of course a way to escape
one night when the fog is at its peak
I shall slip the cowl of my black cape
low over my eyes
and when I'm too far away
for him to remember how my hips
melt into his hands
I'll write a letter unsigned
disguising the way pain
has drawn my lips into a cruel smile
or how I must now use men
for what they are
and never what I imagined him to be

The Dragon Lady Considers Dinner

the next day I couldn't remember his name
there was that business with the flaming crepes
and the sea breaking around them
my fingers played a tattoo of ancient melodies
the oysters passed the tune to the lobsters
under the straw pattern of my wide black bamboo hat
I picked carrion from my teeth
it was all so boring
no amount of voodoo could save me
I dreamed of ghettos in revolution
he talked of contracts and commodities
I smiled at the oysters
they didn't smile back
the butter ran silently along the spine

he promised gold and all the exotic pelts
the world could offer
now more than ever I needed the loan
of his fleet of ships and long guns
I told him a lady flies low
and manages her own power
the sun nodded its approval
the waiter poured more wine
I wiped my lips pausing
as I rose to leave
the oysters chuckled inside me

The Dragon Lady Meets Her Match

there are those who would tell you
it was the man with the black mustache
his insouciant charm stripping
away my mask like confetti
but in reality it was Nefertiti and Sheba
who taught me the Nubian secrets of movements
fluid and balanced as lines of poetry
or a flashing machete lovely as diamonds
and faceted to suit the mood

because gossip keeps the fires bright
I still hear stories of the Mongolian
how he churned the waters
until gunboats tipped
into my lap like roses
but this is only a tale
for what man has not been subdued
by the tides of the moon or woman
lured by a postcard expanse of wilderness

what are the choices
a network of lace and spatulas
to keep you bedded and knee-deep in diapers
I prefer to fill my hands with maps
and weapons fit for ladies of royalty
I have flirted with armies of handsome fools
like Princess Littlefeather or Catherine
the Great who defied the convention
of quietly sitting with knees together

it is true that I have fallen prey
to the plots of crackerjack pilots
who knew all too well how to read my heart
on nights filled with the dim light
of a lonely moon they have painted
the enchantment in my eyes
but my real fate comes with the likes
of Sierra Rose, Sojourner and Cattle Kate
those women who never learned
to corset their actions
or know who can properly bow
from the waist

I have studied the acts of warrior ladies
twice they've brought me back to life
pulling the murderous tip
of some lover's secret weapon from my breasts
each time I have patched the brittle edges
each time it has altered my course
but we are products of our imaginations
and love is a fragile shell we cross
inviting mistakes
it is a matter of timing
and I the judge will be the loser

The Dragon Lady Speaks of Celibacy

paint a canvas of surreal memories
you are the artist always in control

regale your friends with stories of abuse
you are the world's champion victim

remember your lover's every nuance and gesture
trace every incident that led to your disaster

listen to any and all disgusting offers
you're more amused than impressed by prosaic recitals

make no plans longer than twenty-four hours in advance
all of which require more money than you'll ever have on hand

attack your memories with all the adrenaline you can muster
stay young inside one love-from-afar affair per year

build well-seasoned houses with broth and stew
learn when to do from scratch and when to make do

develop the smugness of your own personal mystery
this is the calligraphy of being alone

Biography: 1936 to War's End

first it was the gunboats
the occasional bursts of small-arms fire
then jets and choppers
and those awful supermarket women
squawking like magpies
and the fields littered with grim-faced
farmers wondering how a woman could know
so much

they called me names
Lady of the Inferno
Woman of Dragon's Tongue
Black Witch of the Orient
and on every horizon
I found a line of pilots and pirates
waiting to trail me
for a buck and a quarter

I just grew weary of the whole game
pulled on my boots and marched
right out front where I could face them
in no time at all had their attention
maybe because I stood there
sleek in my black cape and ruby-red
fingernails ready for action

I tell them Hong Kong or St. Louis
it's all the same
they say ladies like me
are no longer needed
be feminine they say
they say peace will come soon
they say tomorrow marks
the end of the century

I hear the battle
drawing nearer

The Dragon Lady's Legacy

years later, they could hardly remember her face
then a farmer plowing a tired field of soybeans
and lentils near Half Moon Bay
found her pearl-handled revolver
in a sump by a forgotted wellhouse
silt slid from the curve of metal
like folds in a silk dress and her initials
filled the dreary light with promise

for days, he carried the secret in his pocket
then his dreams infected his wife
she saw fires scorching the villages
in the valleys below them
the smell of strangers grew thick as napalm
and a slit of light, crafty as a woman's sigh
suggested battles yet to be planned
somewhere in the night she heard the lady speak

your breath will pulse in strobe-light patterns
of eight, she whispered
two for your husband and unnamed children
one for this house teetering
on its crumbling foundation like a child
one for that useless fence and barn
another for your sisters in other ghettos
the rest for yourself arising
gloriously, finally a rebel
alive outside yourself

each night, the lady returned
the farmer bathed himself in tales of love
where he was the hero
his wife pressed her onion-stained fingers
to her ears and begged for the old loneliness
the days pale as thin soup
the brief spate of evenings
still she saw the variegated shadows of sandalwood
so surprisingly delicate the lady took shape in them

her razor-sharp nails glistening like diamonds
come follow me, she said
it is an old story so foreign
it is typically Middle American, as always
when it is finally released to the public
everyone from lawyers to victims
will be FBI agents
but you are full of long-limbed seduction
and have nothing to fear

even now, soothed by the swell of adventure
there are those who say the lady is a myth
in these days there is no siren's voice
to lure men into battle or women
from the quicksand of supermarkets
there are no ladies of iron will or dark mysteries
and when you have settled into the safe corral
of your routine, *do not be deceived*
by the faint scent of our perfume

About the Author:

Colleen McElroy has been a speech therapist, a talk-show moderator, a poet and short story writer, and a professor of writing, literature, and women's studies. A graduate of the University of Washington (Ph.D. 1973), McElroy has received an N.E.A. fellowship and a *Push-cart: Best of Small Presses* award. Her previous books are: *Lie and Say You Love Me, Winters Without Snow, Music From Home: Selected Poems,* and *The Mules Done Long Since Gone.* She is professor of English at the University of Washington and lives in Seattle.

About the Book:

The illustrations on pages i, iii, 1, 11, 21, 23, 33, 34, 35, 45 and 72 are line adaptations of prehistoric art. The illustrations on pages 51, 57, 58, 63 and 80 are line adaptations of early African art.

The text is set in Friz Quadrata by Marathon Typography Service, Durham, North Carolina.

The printing and binding is by Thomson-Shore, Dexter, Michigan on 60 lb. Warren's Olde Style.

Design by Joyce Kachergis.